THE STATUE OF LIBERTY

A History and
A Celebration

THE STATUE OF LIBERTY

A History and A Celebration

BY MAUREEN HEFFERNAN

Woodbury Press

ISBN 0-8081-6279-9

THE STATUE OF LIBERTY: A History and a Celebration
was prepared and produced by
Patti Cake Productions
P.O. Box 38
Durham, North Carolina 27701

Color separations by Hong Kong Scanner Craft Company, Ltd.
Printed and bound in Hong Kong by Leefung-Asco Printers, Ltd.

Woodbury Press is an exclusive imprint of
B. Dalton Bookseller, Minneapolis, Minnesota.

ACKNOWLEDGMENTS

In researching *The Statue of Liberty,* I depended on the following books: *The Statue of Liberty* by Marvin Trachtenberg; *Statue of Liberty: the First Hundred Years* by Bernard Weisberger; *In Search of Liberty* by James B. Bell and Richard I. Abrams; *The Statue of Liberty* by Charles Mercer; *I Lift My Lamp* by Hertha Pauli and E.B. Ashton, and *The Statue of Liberty* by Michael George.

I would also like to thank for their substantial and much appreciated help Felecia Abbadessa, Louise Quayle, Mary Moriarty, Christine Cancelli, Dick Boddy and Alison Lee. Special thanks to Susan Duane for her help in gathering the photos; to Allan Lang and to Chris Mosley.

INTRODUCTION

Just a short distance away from Manhattan's jagged and hard-edged profusion of towers rises, in graceful and harmonious contrast, the form of a colossal robed woman. The Statue of Liberty has stood here for one hundred years.

Two million people visit her annually. From all parts of the country and the world they arrive, to marvel at her heroic size and imposing, eloquent beauty, to reflect on the promise she embodies, and in the case of many Americans, to imagine that moment when immigrant forebears arriving by boat first caught sight of the statue— their welcome into the New World.

She has served in her hundred-year history as "mother of exiles," propagandistic device, commercial logo, and the butt of artistic jokes. Despite the varied and sometimes ignoble ways in which her image has been used, the Statue of Liberty remains as powerful and treasured a symbol of America as the flag.

Liberty's calm gaze and serene posture carry little hint of the struggle that attended her creation. How after twenty years of effort and in the face of almost incredible odds, the dedication of a talented few and the generosity of the masses enabled to be built the most famous statue in the world is a story as remarkable as the Statue of Liberty herself.

CHAPTER 1

A FAMOUS DINNER PARTY

The Statue of Liberty was born out of one of the most troubled times in French history. France in the mid-1800s was a country struggling to find government which would endure. The bloody revolution of 1789 was fresh in the minds of its citizens and the dismantling of the guillotine did not end the turbulent atmosphere. Napoléon Bonaparte, who rose to power in the revolution's aftermath, created a French empire that stretched across Europe—only to lose it at the hands of the British and Germans. Emperor Napoléon III proved a vain, repressive ruler who would lead the country into war with Germany—a military disaster for France that would cost it the provinces of Alsace and Lorraine. While one government after another grappled with the power that had come to it, the intellectuals and philosophers of France—indeed, of all Europe—anxiously watched the young republic

Just off the boat. Some 50 million have taken the short ferry ride to Liberty Island and the Statue.

across the Atlantic that was founded on the same enlightened and democratic ideals that inspired the French Revolution of 1789. Would the American experiment succeed or would its government be torn apart in civil war? If democracy could prevail in the United States, its establishment in Europe was only a matter of time—or so ran the thinking of the French *philosophes*.

★ ★ ★

It was in this political climate that Édouard-René Lefebvre de Laboulaye, legal scholar and the author of a three-volume work on the United States, gathered together a distinguished group of political thinkers and writers for dinner one evening in 1865. The subject of their conversation was sympathy between countries, in particular

During World War I, the Statue of Liberty served as theme and symbol for the Liberty Loan drives, which were launched by the U.S. Department of the Treasury to raise money for the war.

the longstanding friendship between France and the United States. Here, noted Laboulaye, were two countries united by similar ideas and aspirations, whose soldiers had fought together during the American War of Independence. "If a monument were to be built in America as a memorial to their independence," he said, "I should think it very natural if it were built by united efforts, if it were a common work of both nations."

★ ★ ★

By today's standards, when high-interest loans, weapons, and grain surpluses are thought to be appropriate donations to friendly countries, Laboulaye's idea for the gift of a big statue seems wildly romantic—the fact that he and his colleagues moved the people of two countries to actually erect the Statue of Liberty is a modern

miracle. Two things, however, must be remembered: Laboulaye and his contemporaries lived during a time when building monuments was a popular form of artistic expression in all the cities of Europe; and Laboulaye's circle was motivated by more than simple generosity. Laboulaye had hit upon an idea both inspired and shrewd. The creators of the Statue of Liberty doubtless acted out of sincere admiration for the United States and a real wish to celebrate the new nation's accomplishment. At the same time, however, they knew that a public campaign to build a monument to liberty in America was an exceedingly happy plan to promote the idea of liberty in France. Fortunately, Laboulaye had addressed his remarks to a man well-suited to execute so grandiose an idea, the sculptor Frédéric Auguste Bartholdi.

CHAPTER 2

BARTHOLDI

Colossal statuary exerted a mighty grip on the imagination of the sculptor Bartholdi. Born in 1834 in the Alsatian town of Colmar, France, he had already won a name for himself at the age of 19. His first major work, a statue of a local military hero under Napoléon Bonaparte, General Jean Rapp, received all the more critical and popular attention because at twenty-six feet high, it was too big to fit inside the exhibition hall of the Paris Salon of 1855 and had to be repositioned—very advantageously—directly outside the door.

In Bartholdi's time heroically scaled statues were not at all uncommon. The mid-nineteenth century was the great age of monument building. Ushered in by the Industrial Revolution and the new wealth and materialism it fostered, a continuous parade of statues issued forth from sculpture studios of Europe. All the statues more or less

The caption in this 1884 picture reads "The Gift of France to the American People. THE BARTHOLDI COLOSSAL STATUE, Liberty Enlightening the World."

conformed to the classical style inherited from ancient Greece and Rome. Usually they commemorated national heroes and heroines or idealized such notions as Truth, Virtue, Commerce and the Arts.

Bartholdi, by nature enthusiastic and ambitious, wanted to take the art further: He wanted to build sculpture of truly monumental scale, towering figures reminiscent of the legendary Colossus of Rhodes and the Parthenon Athena, immortalized in the writings of the ancients.

A trip to Egypt in 1856 with several of his artist friends brought Bartholdi face to face with the kind of monument he dreamed of creating himself. When the group visited the Sphinx and the Pyramids, Bartholdi was overwhelmed. So powerful was the impression the Egyptian ruins made on the young man, he could still write

F. A. Bartholdi, Statue of Liberty Sculptor

1985 commemorative postage stamp honoring the Statue of Liberty and Bartholdi.

some thirty years later, "We are filled with profound emotion in the presence of these colossal witnesses, centuries old, of a past that to us is almost infinite, at whose feet so many generations, so many million existences, so many human glories have rolled in the dust." Here in the Egyptian colossi was a perfectly realized ideal of grandeur and solemnity that Bartholdi would strive to match in his own work.

★ ★ ★

When Laboulaye first suggested a monument celebrating American liberty, Bartholdi couldn't wait to begin. Laboulaye, while encouraging his friend, knew he would have to keep him in check. In 1865, the repressive Second Empire still controlled France. Laboulaye realized that if he were to make public a scheme requiring

Statue of Lafayette by Bartholdi, Union Square, New York City. Bartholdi's earlier sculpture was commissioned by French republicans as a gift to the city. It honored New Yorkers who had generously aided the French during the Franco-Prussian War. The statue of Lafayette, hero during the American War of Independence and friend of George Washington, memorialized the long history of friendship uniting America and France.

In this early engraving Liberty looms against a busy metropolitan background. Behind her Jersey City, Manhattan, Brooklyn and the Hudson and East rivers stretch into the distance.

nationwide support that carried the message of liberty, Napoléon III would put a quick stop to the effort. They would have to wait for a more propitious moment to launch their plan.

Bartholdi busied himself with other projects. He maintained one studio in Paris and another in his native Colmar where he was able to spend time with his mother Charlotte Bartholdi, to whom the young sculptor was exceptionally close. Commuting by train back and forth between Paris and Alsace, he could enjoy Parisian gaiety and bustle and when he had had his fill, he could repair to the quiet streets of Colmar with their picturesque old burghers' houses. It must have been a pleasant life.

This tranquil way of life ended when, in 1870, Napoléon III launched an ill-advised war against Germany.

France expected to meet little resistance, but the better-trained German army managed to turn the tables on the poorly equipped, poorly led French troops. As a victory prize, Germany annexed Alsace and Lorraine and levied a back-breaking financial penalty against the French people. Bartholdi himself watched German soldiers advance on Colmar; he felt bitterly the humiliation of defeat and loss of his homeland.

★ ★ ★

In the spring of 1871, Bartholdi once again attended a gathering at the home of Édouard de Laboulaye. Laboulaye sensed in the prevailing discontent and chaos that the time had come to take another step in the Liberty project, and he proposed that Bartholdi make a trip to the United States.

Bartholdi found an ideal site for his statue in the parade ground within the star-shaped Fort Wood on Bedloe's Island.

"Go to see that country," he urged, "You will study it; you will bring back to us your impressions. Propose to our friends over there to make with us a monument, a common work, in remembrance of the ancient friendship of France and the United States. We will take up a subscription in France. If you find a happy idea, a plan that will excite public enthusiasm, we are convinced that it will be successful on both continents, and we will do a work that will have a far-reaching moral effect."

"It was then," Bartholdi recalled many years later, "that the germ of the monument of the French-American Union was found."

CHAPTER 3

A VISIT TO AMERICA

Bartholdi departed for New York aboard the steamship *Pereire* on June 8, 1871. His goals were to come up with a concept for the monument and to find an appropriate site. During the thirteen-day voyage he sketched furiously in his search for a noble and immortal image to embody liberty. Its precise shape eluded him until June 21st, when the boat entered the Narrows of New York harbor.

"The picture that is presented to view when one arrives at New York is marvelous," he later wrote, "when...in the pearly radiance of a beautiful morning is revealed the magnificent spectacle of those immense cities, of those rivers extending as far as the eye can reach, festooned with masts and flags; when one awakes, so to speak, in the midst of that interior sea covered with vessels, some giant in size, some dwarfs, which swarm

about, puffing, whistling, swinging the great arms of their uncovered walking-beams, moving to and fro like a crowd upon a public place.''

The Frenchman was decided at once: he would build his monument here, at the entrance to the New World and on the threshold of that mighty city that gave most visitors their first experience of America. According to Bartholdi, he sketched out a robed woman raising a torch to liberty as soon as his ship entered the bay.

Another goal of Bartholdi's mission was to win support for the Liberty monument in America. In fact, Laboulaye could not have found an emissary better suited to the task of advance promotion for Liberty than its creator. However debatable Bartholdi's talents as a sculptor—and they have been widely disputed—critics are

agreed on one point: he was a superb salesman of his own work. His handsomeness, natural enthusiasm and energy, gregariousness and absolute confidence—plus a tremendous drive to accomplish whatever he undertook—made him highly effective when it came time to turn listeners into sponsors.

Laboulaye had wisely furnished his friend with letters of introduction to some of the United States' most prominent and influential citizens. Bartholdi spent the first few weeks of his stay making connections in the Eastern Seaboard cities where the established elite resided. In New York he met with Horace Greeley, editor of the *New York Tribune*, and George William Curtis, editor of *Harper's Weekly*, in Boston, Henry Wadsworth Longfellow; in Washington, Senator Charles Sumner of Massachusetts; in Newport, Rhode Island, the architect

The Statue of Liberty plays prominently in this Liberty Loan poster for 1917. Aimed at recent immigrants, it urges them to "remember" their adopted country by contributing to the war effort.

Richard Morris Hunt's design for the pedestal.

Richard Morris Hunt (who, it turned out, would later design the statue's pedestal).

Bartholdi also made the trip to the summer White House in Long Branch, New Jersey, where he introduced himself to President Ulysses S. Grant. Unfortunately, the sculptor was unable to interest President Grant in his idea.

The sculptor set off cross country by train in August, 1871, visiting Niagara Falls, Detroit, Omaha, Salt Lake City (where he met the Mormon leader Brigham Young) and San Francisco. On his way back east, he stopped in Denver, St. Louis and Cincinnati. As a member of Laboulaye's circle—and therefore a faithful supporter of the Union—he would not, however, set foot below the Mason-Dixon line.

"Everything here is big," he wrote to Laboulaye, describing the feature of America which impressed him

Liberty's completed head displayed at the Paris Universal Exposition of 1878.

most forcibly during that trip. In its bigness he perceived a crucial difference between the United States and France: here was no tight-knit, homogeneous country but a vast, wild land inhabited by pockets of people as cut off from each other as if they had been separated by oceans. How would he ever be able to unite them behind his project? Despite this question, Bartholdi sent to Laboulaye an optimistic report:

"In every town I look for people who may wish to take part in my enterprise. So far I have found them everywhere; the ground is well-prepared; only the spark will have to be provided by a manifestation on the part of France."

CHAPTER 4

A GODDESS NAMED LIBERTY

Once back in his Paris studio, Bartholdi continued work on the statue's design. The concept itself, a heroically scaled woman, erected near a great waterway with a torch raised in one hand, was not entirely new to the sculptor when he first beheld America from aboard the *Pereire*. It almost certainly evolved from an earlier project, conceived during his trip to Egypt. While travelling, Bartholdi had met another Frenchman with big ideas, Ferdinand de Lesseps, builder of the Suez Canal. Inspired by his countryman's engineering feat, Bartholdi proposed that a lighthouse—reminiscent of the legendary Lighthouse of Alexandria, one of the Seven Wonders of the Ancient World—be raised at the entrance to Suez. This structure would take the shape of a colossal female *fellah*, or Egyptian peasant, bearing a torch. "Egypt Carrying the Light to Asia" never went up, however, as

Bartholdi was unable to find a backer. The project only got as far as a few sketches and models.

The similarity of these early models to the finished Statue of Liberty is persuasive evidence that Bartholdi drew upon his earlier work when he produced his final design. Bartholdi would never admit the connection, however, as he considered any suggestion of one a slur.

In any event, the sculptor's next task was to refine his concept. For this, Bartholdi relied on his training and looked to the artistic conventions of the day for inspiration. He had been schooled in the neoclassical style—hence Liberty would have idealized features and appear in classical dress. Liberty, as depicted in Eugène Delacroix's painting *Liberty Guiding the People*, showed a robust, bare-breasted woman, flying the French

A dramatic presence at night, spotlit from below.

Tricolor in one hand and brandishing a flintlock gun in the other, charging forward with her compatriots over a mound of corpses. Although this image of Liberty influenced Bartholdi, he shied away from this earthy rendition with its overtones of anarchy and violence—his was a much more formal and self-contained goddess.

The identity and message conveyed by Liberty were drawn from a vocabulary of symbols used by artists over the ages to enrich the meaning of their paintings, sculptures, and monuments. Broken shackles at Liberty's feet pointed to her new, hard-won freedom. A tablet in her left hand, recalling the tablets of Moses, commanded viewers to remember the date inscribed—July IV MDCCLXXVI—the date the Declaration of Independence was signed. The tablet in her left hand served to balance her upheld right hand that held an illuminating beacon.

An early terracotta model by Bartholdi. In this version
Liberty twists emphatically to the right and flings her left
arm backward. The left hand holds a broken vase, ancient
symbol of freedom.

Bartholdi was careful to distinguish this torch from the incendiary torch symbolic of revolution.

On her head, the sculptor placed a radiant seven-spiked crown said to represent the seven continents and seven seas. Here Bartholdi deliberately bypassed convention: most representations of Liberty showed her wearing the Phrygian cap, a headdress given to freed slaves in ancient Rome to signal their new status. This age-old emblem of liberation, however, had become identified with the French Revolution, and was often used in artistic renderings of the liberation of the masses. The symbol's radical overtones, plus the somewhat ungainly shape of the cap, was reason enough for Bartholdi to reject it and substitute the more serene and neutral crown.

Bartholdi modelled the face and figure of the Statue of Liberty after the two women in his life. He is said to

have used his future wife Jeanne-Emilie Baheux de Puysieux as a model for the body and arms. The face he modeled after his mother's—and one wonders how Jeanne-Emilie liked that. A comparison of the statue's visage to photographs of Charlotte Bartholdi shows a clear resemblance. The hard set of Madame's features (she was apparently a cold and disagreeable woman to everyone but her son) are interpreted as symbols of moral fortitude and determination in the statue.

Bartholdi made a shrewd artistic choice when he chose the older woman as a model. He wanted the face of Liberty to be beautiful—and it is. The point is, however, that Bartholdi chose a severe beauty, born of suffering and triumph, which he saw in his mother's face, over Jeanne-Emilie's youthful and untroubled loveliness.

Art historian and critic Marvin Trachtenberg, whose *The Statue of Liberty* is one of the most informative books on the subject, has written that there were some aspects of colossal art that were irresistible to Bartholdi's Romantic sensibility. Its "awesome nature and suitability for 'sublime' natural settings" was part of his interest in this art form, but the real attraction for Bartholdi was in the sheer difficulty of putting it up and making it stand, the triumph of accomplishing this feat, even the ignominy which awaited he who failed. With the form and details of Liberty firmly in mind, Bartholdi had a daunting technical challenge to address.

The materials that would be used to construct the statue were of primary concern and Bartholdi had given them considerable thought. Stone was out of the question for a work of Liberty's size as it presented tremendous

Two colossal New York landmarks, the Statue of Liberty and the twin towers of the World Trade Center.

logistical problems. He rejected bronze as too heavy and too costly. The medium had to be light and malleable.

In his earlier travels, Bartholdi had seen and studied a seventy-five foot statue of St. Charles Borromeo set above Lake Maggiore near Milan. The sculptor Giovanni Battista Crespi had shaped his statue, the largest one existing in Bartholdi's day, out of thin sheets of hammered copper which were then joined and held erect by an interior masonry pier. Bartholdi was not at all impressed by St. Charles Borromeo itself and dismissed it as an "ordinary statue enlarged," possessing little of the majesty and mystery of truly colossal art. Nevertheless, its copper *repoussé* construction gave Bartholdi the answer he was looking for. Hammered copper was light, easy to work with, and would answer the problems raised in erecting such a large statue.

The next formidable dilemma was to devise a structure strong enough to support Liberty. Bartholdi knew he would need assistance here, and he was eventually able to secure the help of engineer Alexandre Gustave Eiffel. Eiffel was chiefly known at the time for his railroad bridges, aqueducts and soaring futuristic steel structures of spidery design and tremendous strength. The Parisian tower he is best known for was built much later. Eiffel, like Bartholdi, was one who relished a professional challenge. He would design a wrought iron skeleton, with a spine of four connected central girders and a lighter framework conformed to the shape of the statue's copper shell. The interior structure would give the statue sufficient support to carry not only its own enormous weight (225 tons) but to withstand the force of heavy winds blowing off the Atlantic.

Liberty rises in the courtyard of the studio of Gaget, Gauthier and Company in Paris.

It had taken Auguste Bartholdi four years to get to this point, from his initial sketch of Liberty as he sailed into New York harbor to the stage where the idea was ready for execution. By 1875, an approved design was in hand and the final plaster model had been cast. A workable material and technique had been found, and the celebrated Parisian workshop of Gaget, Gauthier and Company was ready to begin construction. Only one thing was lacking: money. Although Bartholdi, Laboulaye, and the rest of Liberty's sponsors had, through diligence, ingenuity and patience, overcome one problem after another in bringing Liberty to the launch stage, they could not at this point sense that the most difficult challenge of all lay ahead: how to keep the funds rolling in.

CHAPTER 5

AN APPEAL TO THE PEOPLE

Laboulaye organized in 1875 the Franco-American Union, which acted as the official French administrative organization to erect the Statue of Liberty. It was agreed by the committee that the French would pay for the statue itself; the Americans would be asked to provide a site and bear the expense of the foundation and pedestal. The first public fund-raising appeal was printed on September 28, 1875 in two French newspapers. "In the middle of New York harbor on a little island," it proposed, "will be raised a colossal statue horizoned by the large cities of New York, Jersey City and Brooklyn. On the threshold of that vast continent, full of new life, where ships meet from all parts of the world, it will appear to spring up from the bosom of the waves representing *Liberty Enlightening the World*." Six hundred thousand francs were needed.

The initial French response was encouraging—even though Laboulaye's committee would have to rack their brains for a way to keep up public interest and generosity—and the French campaign sustained enough momentum to allow the actual work on the statue to progress, if slowly. The Franco-American Union staged a sumptuous banquet, a musical benefit, exhibitions, and finally a lottery to raise the required sum. When contributions slowed after the first good showing, Bartholdi came to the rescue with a brilliant strategy aimed at the business sector: for a donation, merchants and manufacturers could obtain the right to reproduce the Statue of Liberty in advertisements of their products. Apparently, French merchants saw a good thing in the picture of a woman named "Liberty;" the scheme succeeded and money flowed in once more.

Full-scale model of the Statue's left arm and hand, executed in wood and plaster. Bartholdi stands below, second from right.

In the studio of Gaget, Gauthier, the complicated procedure of constructing Liberty was underway. From the study model Bartholdi had cast, he remade a plaster model standing one-sixteenth the projected size of the final statue. This was gradually enlarged and adjusted until a satisfactory one-quarter size model was completed. The one-quarter scale model was divided into sections, which were in turn enlarged to four times their size to create full scale plaster sections. Wooden molds were then constructed around the plaster forms, that took an exact impression of their every bend and fold. Next, craftsmen removed the wooden molds and hammered into them thin sheets of copper. When complete, the copper sheeting exactly reproduced the shapes of the full-scale plaster forms. These thin copper pieces—numbering 300 in total—were finally ready to be riveted together to form the

Craftsmen hammering copper sheets inside the studio of Gaget, Gauthier. They look lilliputian against the enormous plaster arm and hand behind them.

skin of the statue and to be joined to Eiffel's supporting metal trusswork. Work began in 1876 and the colossus finally stood complete in the courtyard of Gaget, Gauthier in 1884, after an eight year effort.

In its first year, however, Liberty's French sponsors began to perceive their gift to the American people would not be received with the same warmth that attended its creation.

America's lack of interest first showed up in the government's reluctance to act on the project. Although Laboulaye's request for a site was presented to President Grant in late 1875, no action was taken nor did any fund-raising committee yet exist to parallel the efforts of the Franco-American Union in France. The American response, as it was echoed in the press, was often either disbelieving or critical. Newspaper editorials dismissed

Huge fragments of Liberty patiently await the trial assembly of the statue in the courtyard of Gaget, Gauthier.

An amused Frenchman poses between the toes.

the project as wild French folly, poked fun at Bartholdi's design, violently objected to American participation in the cost, or all three.

Today, the thought that our glorious national monument was actually not wanted and quite nearly turned back by the American public of 1875 seems close to sacrilege. How could Americans not have wanted this gift? What would New York harbor be without her? That late nineteenth century immigrants could have landed in New York without Liberty there to welcome them is almost impossible to imagine.

In the context of the times, however, American resistance is easier to understand. In the 1870s, the Statue of Liberty possessed none of the patriotic or sentimental significance we attach to it today. The statue existed only in

Halfway there. Eiffel's delicate-looking yet immensely strong armature shows above the statue's copper shell.

sketches and small models; few Americans believed it could be realized. The dream originated in France, all of the momentum was in France, and the reverberations of a monument to liberty were more deeply felt in France. The struggle for liberty there was very much alive, whereas the United States, having just survived civil war and economic depression, was preoccupied with its own recovery. Moreover, there was the heavy cost of the pedestal to consider, and the American public simply found it hard to digest the news that it was required to raise and spend $100,000 merely to erect a pedestal. A $100,000 *pedestal?*

Also coming into play was the familiar antagonism of the rest of the country towards New York City. Why, reasoned critics who chose this line of attack, should the entire country bear the expense of a monument that

An 1884 painting by Victor Dargaud shows Liberty standing like a giantess above the streets of Paris.

would be enjoyed mainly by New Yorkers? Let the rich of New York pay the price! They certainly could afford it.

Despite the wall of indifference, Bartholdi and the French-American Union pressed ahead. The American Centennial was near. The committee reckoned the best way to arouse interest and support was actually to send over to the United States a finished portion of the statue, and give the public a taste of what it would be getting in hopes that it would pay for more. Bartholdi rushed to complete the hand and torch, which were shipped and caused much commotion at the Philadelphia Exposition of 1876.

An American organizing committee was at last formed in 1877 and was presided over by William M. Evarts, a former Secretary of State. The committee took strides in securing Congress's approval of the Bedloe's Island site,

The statue's torch-bearing hand is displayed at the Phila-delphia Exposition of 1876.

in choosing the talented Richard M. Hunt as architect of the pedestal, and in appointing General Charles Stone to supervise work on the foundation. Both men were as perfectly suited to their roles as Bartholdi and Eiffel were to theirs. Stone was an able organizer and engineer. Hunt's noble pedestal would manage both to balance and to enhance the beauty of the statue above it.

Lack of cash, however, still threatened to bring down the curtain on the entire project. Evart's committee worked over the course of the next six years to raise the money, but finally realized that contributions from civic groups and schools, or funds raised through benefits and fairs, would only go so far. Clearly, a few sizable checks were needed from captains of industry or a large grant from the government. No wealthy benefactor

materialized, and Congress turned a deaf ear to all appeals for money. By 1885 all that appeared of the pedestal was a few courses of stone; no further source of revenues was in sight. On March 10th, Evarts ordered work stopped.

Salvation came from an unforeseen quarter. Joseph Pulitzer, publisher of the New York *World* had learned of Lady Liberty's plight. Pulitzer was yet another larger-than-life nineteenth-century figure; like de Lesseps, Eiffel and Bartholdi he was a combustible mix of drive, nerve, talent and vision. Having immigrated into this country in 1864, he had quickly made his fortune as publisher of *The St. Louis Post-Dispatch*, which he built into one of the most influential and respected of Midwestern newspapers. By 1883, Pulitzer was ready to take on the capital of

Within the image:
© MOLE & THOMAS
915 MEDINAH BLDG.
CHICAGO, ILL.

HUMAN STATUE OF LIE
18,000 OFFICERS AND M
AT
CAMP DODGE, DES MOINB
COL. WM. NEWMAN, COMMAN
COL. RUSH S. WELLS, DIRECT

An artistic assembly of 18,000 soldiers at Camp Dodge in Des Moines.

An early 20th century postcard.

American journalism and he purchased the *World*, one of New York's lesser papers, meaning to revitalize it.

In the Liberty campaign's flailing efforts, Pulitzer saw a scenario tailor-made to appeal to the minds and hearts of New York's working people, his targeted audience for the *World*. Pulitzer determined that he, his paper and its readers would rescue the Statue of Liberty. By linking the *World* to the Liberty cause, he would also, and not incidentally, sell more newspapers. (By the end of the five-month drive, the *World* would enjoy the largest circulation in the Western hemisphere.)

Pulitzer's paper launched one fund-raising campaign in 1883—unsuccessfully—and another on March 15, 1885. That day, Pulitzer opened his second drive with a resounding appeal.

"Money must be raised to complete the pedestal for the Bartholdi Statue. It would be an irrevocable disgrace to New York City and the American Republic to have France send this splendid gift without our having provided even so much as a landing place for it...The statue is now completed and ready to be brought over to our shores...Congress, by a refusal to appropriate the necessary money to complete preparations for its proper reception and erection, has thrown the responsibility back to the American people. There is but one thing that can be done. *We must raise the money!* The *World* is the people's paper, and it now appeals to the people to come forward and raise the money. The $250,000 that the making of the statue cost was paid in by the masses of the French people, by the workingmen, the

The logo of the 1986 Statue of Liberty Ellis Island Centennial decorates this enamel box.

tradesmen, the shop girls, the artisians...Let us respond in that manner. Let us not wait for the millionaires to give this money. It is not a gift from the millionaires of France to the millionaires of America, but a gift of the whole people of France to the whole people of America. Take this appeal to yourself personally. It is meant for every reader of the *World*. Giving something, however little...We will receive it, and see that it is properly applied. We will also publish the name of every giver, however small the sum given. Let us hear from the people.''

A goal of $100,000 was set.

Miraculously, the strategy worked. Money flowed in, most of it in very small amounts. Civic groups, school

Liberty encased. The 1986 restoration progresses.

children, immigrants, employees of large companies, Grand Army of the Republic posts, men and women young and old sent in their "mites," as individuals often termed their penny, dime and dollar contributions. The *World* faithfully printed the name of every donor. At the end of only two months, its coffers contained $52,203.41, half the sum needed to complete the pedestal. Evart's committee could now order work on the base to begin again.

Meanwhile, in France, Laboulaye and his colleagues had spent numerous anxious moments wondering if the Americans would live up to their side of the bargain. Seeing the *World's* success so far, they could heave a tentative sigh of relief, and preparations to transport Liberty to New York began. Two hundred fourteen crates containing the dismantled statue were carried by rail from Paris to Rouen, a port city of the Seine, and loaded onto

the French naval transport *Isere*. The *Isere* set sail on May 21, 1885 and arrived in New York June 17th. New York greeted the boat in a spirit of high anticipation (the public indifference that had so long prevailed seemed now to have completely disappeared) and fêted the *Isere's* crew with a parade and an official welcome at City Hall.

The statue's arrival pumped even more steam into the *World's* drive for funds, and on August 11, 1885, it announced: ''ONE HUNDRED THOUSAND DOLLARS! TRIUMPHANT COMPLETION OF THE WORLD'S FUND FOR THE LIBERTY PEDESTAL.'' 120,000 individuals from all over the country had contributed, making the Statue of Liberty a true work of the people in America as it had been in France. Laboulaye's original vision, a monument to liberty erected by the people of two friendly nations, had indeed been realized.

CHAPTER 6

A SYMBOL LIVES FOREVER

Work on the statue now proceeded swiftly; by April 1886 the pedestal was complete and by October, the statue was ready for inauguration. An unveiling date was set: October 28, 1886. That gala day dawned wet and foggy, nevertheless, one million wildly cheering New Yorkers turned out to see the biggest marching parade in New York history and a nautical parade of 300 ships sailing down from 42nd Street to surround Bedloe's Island for the ceremony. After interminable speeches, Bartholdi himself pulled the cord which caused a great tricolor covering Liberty's features to fall away. A huge noise went up the moment the statue's face was revealed: horns and sirens blasted from the boats below, cannons boomed, spectators continued to yell.

Bartholdi returned to France a happy man. It seemed, after all the furious activity and twenty years of effort,

Inauguration Day, October 28, 1886. A naval artillery salute veils the statue in smoke.

that the Statue of Liberty would now quietly take her place as guardian of New York's harbor—a dignified reminder of American democracy and freedom and the achievements of the Founding Fathers.

Liberty's historical message, while weighty enough, did not carry much immediacy in the rapidly changing and expanding American society of the late nineteenth century. That the statue did grow into an ever more vital symbol, instead of merely surviving as a somewhat quaint and irrelevant witness to eighteenth century ideals is due to Bartholdi's inspired choice of site. He sensed the importance and drama of the New York port, the entrance to the New World. Whatever happened of significance here would take place literally at the feet of the statue; participants would remember her presence. In particular, she was remembered by the tens of millions of European

Time has been Liberty's most threatening foe. The current restoration will repair damage caused by 100 years of wind, water and salt.

immigrants who arrived in New York during the late 1800s and early 1900s. That the meaning of the statue would become wedded to this great wave of immigration was prophesied in Emma Lazarus's poem of 1883:

Not like the brazen giant of Greek fame,
With conquering limbs astride from land to land;
Here at our sea-washed, sunset gates shall stand
A mighty woman with a torch, whose flame
Is the imprisoned lightning, and her name
Mother of Exiles. From her beacon-hand

Glows world-wide welcome; her mild eyes command
The air-bridged harbor that twin cities frame.
"Keep, ancient lands, your storied pomp!" cries she
With silent lips. "Give me your tired, your poor,
Your huddled masses yearning to breathe free,
The wretched refuse of your teeming shore.
Send these, the homeless, tempest-tost to me.
I lift my lamp beside the golden door!"

John Lennon pleads for peace under Liberty's approving gaze.

Lee Iacocca, Chairman, Statue of Liberty—Ellis Island Centennial Commission.

Liberty's sculptor intended the statue to stand for a thousand years, but he could not protect her from the ravages of weather and pollution. In 1984, after an extensive study by French and American architects and engineers, President Reagan launched an ambitious restoration project to be completed in time for the Statue of Liberty's centennial celebration in 1986. The Statue of Liberty Ellis Island Centennial Commission, presided over by Chrysler chairman Lee Iacocca, is collecting over $230 million to restore and repair the statue and the landmark buildings of Ellis Island, which was the U.S. immigration center between 1892 and 1954.

Liberty is now being overhauled from the spikes of her crown to the bottom of her pedestal, inside and out. The study team of architects found Liberty's interior supporting structure so badly corroded that parts of the statue

Combining modern tools and techniques and Bartholdi's own methods, craftsmen restore the flame of Liberty's torch.

were near collapse; repair involves the replacement of 1,600 iron ribs with handmade stainless steel ones, and the reworking of a weak connection between Liberty's upraised right arm and the central iron pylon. The installment of air conditioning and ventillation will lessen humidity and prevent further interior damage.

Bartholdi's original torch had been remodeled in glass in 1916; the glass torch will now be replaced by a gold-plated flame that duplicates the original version. French artisans from Reims, experts in Bartholdi's own technique of copper *repoussé* construction, are handling the restoration of the statue's copper shell.

Most of the funds have come from corporations, but individuals, schools and patriotic groups have also contributed substantially to the effort. When the facelift is complete, and the scaffolding comes down, the copper

goddess will again be revealed in her original splendor. Such is the enduring romance and appeal of this statue, that for those who have contributed to her 1986 restoration, she is as much a labor of love as she was to those who first created her one hundred years ago.

Photo Credits